Exploring
Cross Stitch

Exploring Cross Stitch
a notebook

Audrey Ormrod

Photography by Dudley Moss

A&C Black · London

Acknowledgments

My first 'thank you' is to my husband,
Bob, who has always been caring and
supportive through failures and successes.
I should also like to thank Anne
Watts, my editor, who has been
enthusiastic since I first showed her
the book and who has made the
whole process so pleasant.
My thanks to Dudley Moss for his excellent
photographs and to the Reading branch
of the Embroiderers' Guild where we learn
from each other, exchange our
'goodies' and make friends.

First published 1988
A & C Black (Publishers) Limited
35 Bedford Row, London WC1R 4JH

ISBN 0–7136–2945–2

© 1988 Audrey Ormrod

British Library Cataloguing in
Publication Data

Ormrod, Audrey
 Exploring cross stitch: a notebook.
 1. Cross-stitch
 I. Title
 746.44   TT778.C76

 ISBN 0–7136–2945–2

Printed in Hong Kong
by Dai Nippon Printing Co. Ltd

Contents

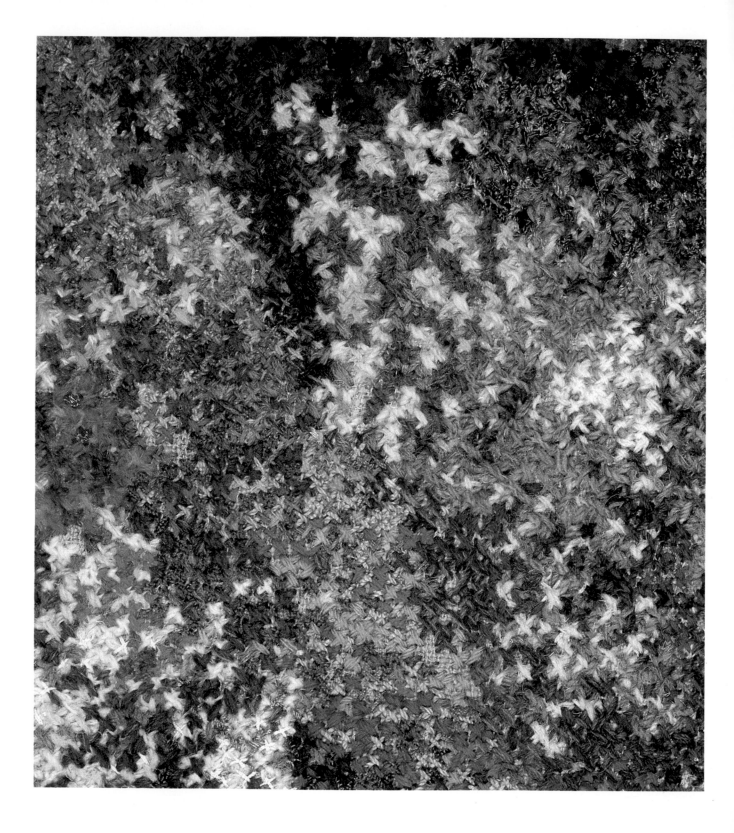

I began cross stitch as a challenge – and a challenge it certainly proved. I gave myself three months to see if I could make it do lively things.

At first it was quite sterile and then a bitter battle started. The crosses were unyielding, they stuck their two little feet in the ground and would not budge. I was unimaginative, unable to forget the traditional concept of cross stitch. I burnt the midnight oil and groaned with frustration – gradually a few small experiments began to come alive and show promise. Then more and more ideas came, in a trickle at first, and then a flow. Our relationship was beginning and I felt a great sense of excitement! I tried faces and figures, trees and fields and the most mobile thing I could think of – a line of washing – and began to find that anything was possible.

At the end of these early experiments I did some larger finished works and realised that the stitch had endless potential and the very rigidity I hated so much at the beginning was showing unique qualities of strength – but much more, stitches could dance all over the fabric as lightly as tossed leaves or could be coerced into flowing lines. They could be delicate, they could be heavy; fine and simple as a Japanese print, bright and strong as a Matisse painting. Ideas were coming in torrents and I suddenly knew that I had reached an important point in my work.

I felt that I was standing in a hall surrounded by lots and lots of doors and behind each was a long corridor. Some doors were now wide open, others were tantalisingly half closed with exciting glimpses of what lay beyond. I wanted to dash in and out of all of them, but embroidery is a slow craft and I had to stop and think carefully which doors to go through first and explore.

At this point I decided to make a notebook.

This notebook shows my own development of the stitch from very basic beginnings to some more adventurous concepts and I hope that it will start a lot of people thinking of cross stitch in a new creative way. Some of the embroideries shown are experimental pieces and they do not always succeed. Nevertheless, the exercise is of benefit for one learns from it.

Throughout the notebook I have concentrated on how I arrived at my designs (often by very simple methods) in order to encourage everyone to try out new ideas. It is very rewarding and exciting.

Although there has been some arranging of the notebook by theme and method, it is basically a progression. The first part shows simple methods of design and of their transfer to fabric; the second part illustrates more experimental exercises and finished works (some of them developed from sketches earlier in the notebook).

I would urge everyone to keep all samples, experiments, drawings and notes: these often prove invaluable in later work. It is also very interesting to look back on one's own development. And do date all your work.

Beginnings

In my earliest experiments I was weighed down with tradition. It never occurred to me to work cross stitch on anything but a counted thread fabric and to make it a square stitch. This blockage held up my progress for a long time. One of the first embroideries to mark a small step forward was the Hut on the Hill.

The *Hut on the Hill* was worked on even-weave linen. For the first time I did not plan it on graph paper but tacked the outline of hill and fields directly onto the fabric, which left the whole approach much freer. It grew into a little sampler, the crosses stitched in as many ways as I could devise. They are irregularly spaced and stitched in a variety of threads from wool to cotton which gives a textured effect.

Next I realised that I was considering only traditional cross stitch subjects. I tried to think of a flowing design – the most unlikely subject that one would associate with cross stitch. The *Line of Washing* was the result. It is not a very lively line of washing, in fact it looks like a damp day when the spinner has packed up, but at this stage I dared not take too many liberties with my crosses!

I worked an experimental *Sampler* on a piece of calico. I tacked some guidelines but soon found them unnecessary. I started embroidering on the left-hand side, stitching with coton à broder in self-coloured thread, keeping the stitches regular and working a traditional design. I was surprised to find how quickly I began to work evenly. Then I made a very laboured and unsuccessful attempt to work freely.

On the right-hand side I began again with a traditional pattern. This time the second block began to be interesting. By the last two I was working freely in cross stitch. It was a breakthrough and I realised that a new exciting field of work had opened up. The form of stitches that developed in the last two blocks was used in many later embroideries.

From this time on I began to realise that cross stitch had no limitations. There were no designs or subjects that could not be considered. The cross that I had been using so self-consciously was capable of expressing more atmosphere and emotion than any other stitch.

Fabrics and threads

The first attempts at stitching on calico opened up new ways of working. From this time my ideas developed in two directions, influenced by the two types of fabric that can be used.

Open-weave fabric
This refers to a fabric where you can clearly see the threads and count them. You put the needle between the threads to form regular crosses. Designs are often worked out on squared paper.

The material may vary from expensive even-weave linen to hessian. I have used canvas, scrim, hopsack, binca and many furnishing fabrics. Anything is suitable as long as you can see the threads distinctly enough to be able to put the needle between them. (Use a blunt tapestry needle to avoid piercing the threads.)

These are the materials for traditional cross stitch but much modern and experimental work can be done on them. There are no 'rules' but in general the effect is more attractive if crosses used as individual stitches are worked the same way throughout, i.e. if the top layer of each cross always lies in the same direction.

Even-weave material is very pleasant to use and, as its name would suggest, gives a perfectly square cross. However, equally good effects can be achieved on less expensive fabrics. In some, the thread may be a little wider in one direction of the weave. This produces a slightly rectangular cross and must be borne in mind if you are working from a design on squared paper – it will make the finished embroidery slightly taller or broader according to your decision. In some furnishings fabrics the threads are textured. This will make the crosses a little irregular but may give interesting results. Scrim is very loosely woven and allows a backing material to show through. Very different effects can be achieved by backgrounds of different colours.

The finer the fabric, the finer the stitching thread should be, but it is essential to experiment to find the most pleasing for each design. For more openly woven fabric, such as binca and canvas, try stitching with not only thick threads but with strips of material.

Make lots of samples and keep them all in a notebook. They build up an invaluable source of reference.

This sample on furnishing fabric has eight stitches each way. It shows how some fabrics may distort the cross slightly.

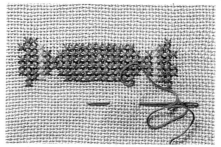

A sweet worked on even-weave, stitched over two threads with a tapestry needle. All the crosses are square and of even size.

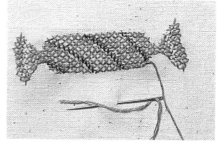

A similar sweet worked quite regularly on calico with a sharp needle. The crosses are judged by eye.

Close-weave fabric

This is a fabric where the structure of the threads can be ignored. The shape, size and placing of the crosses are judged by eye. The stitches can be quite regular or can be used freely in many ways: as a filling stitch or in flowing lines; as single stitches or on top of each other to create tone and texture. Sometimes the stitches are distinct and sometimes not. A sharp needle is needed. I often work crosses with the top threads of the stitch lying the same way, even on close-weave fabric, but sometimes, to create a rougher effect, I stitch in both directions.

I have used calico, denim, dress and furnishing materials, and silk. If the material is fine, it is a good idea to line it and to stitch through both layers to prevent puckering.

Experiment with embroidery threads. Thickness is limited by the tightness of the weave but if the fabric is stretched on a frame and a large needle used it is possible to use thicker thread.

Potter's Store was one of my first pieces of work on a close-weave fabric (calico). I wanted to see how it would look if I worked part of the design in regular stitching and part unevenly to create some texture. One day I caught sight of the inside of a potter's store cupboard: rows of unglazed pots in lovely shapes, all white and smooth with the wall behind very rough. I made templates and tacked the outline of the pots onto the fabric. Except for their patterns the pots are unstitched – it is the shapes in the background stitching that show their form.

Anyone who has not tried working free cross stitch should not be dismissive and think it sloppy or lazy. One has to be just as disciplined to build up texture and colour by piling crosses on top of each other as to work even rows on canvas. The two styles can be equally expressive and both have their place. Free cross stitch is more demanding because one has to think how to place every stitch.

Transferring shapes to fabric

1 On open-weave material

The traditional method for cross stitch design is to work out a plan of the stitches on graph paper. Although it is exciting to find new and freer ways of using the stitch, this can still be a very useful way of designing for some subjects. The following exercise with a horse chestnut leaf shows the stages:

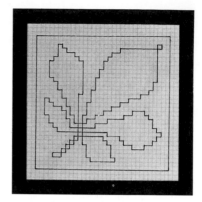

a Photograph of leaf.

b A drawing on graph paper. It can be your own drawing or a tracing.

c The outline is 'squared up' to follow the lines of the graph paper. One square represents one stitch.

d The next stage is to work a small sample of stitches on your fabric. The cross must always be made over at least two threads but may be done over as many as you wish. For a large cross the stitch can be made over several threads of a finer fabric but it is easier to choose a coarser weave and to work over two. The size of the stitch will determine the size of the finished work.

e Copy the design onto the fabric by counting the threads as you stitch. This becomes easy after the first row.

The leaf was designed to fit into a square. It could be used as a repeat pattern or as quarter of a larger square with the leaf facing four ways.

The two embroideries show a difference in scale. The small leaf is stitched in fine thread on even-weave linen. The second is much bolder: stitched in wool on binca. The binca has been mounted on white card which shows through the holes.

2 On close-weave material

Night falls,
My hospice
A cherry tree,
My host
A flower.

This verse by a Japanese poet was my inspiration to work a cherry tree. A tiny piece of deep blue silk decided me to stitch it freely.

The following is a useful method of transferring designs to fabric. It can be exact and detailed or just the minimum of basic lines which leaves the freedom to change and develop the design as it is stitched.

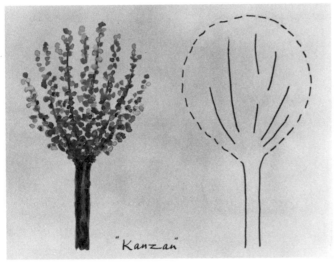

a   b

'My hospice a cherry tree'

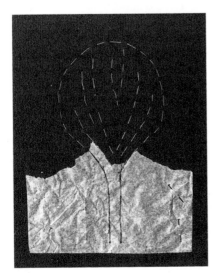

c   d

a Painting of the tree.

b I drew only a few key lines to show the angle of the main branches and the outline of the tree.

c I trace the basic lines onto tissue or tracing paper with a fine ball-point pen and leave to dry. (A pencil leaves black dots on the fabric when you tack through.) Pin paper onto fabric and tack over design lines with small stitches. Then score lines with a needle and gently tear away the paper.

d The embroidery half completed. Remove the tacking stitches as you work – or at the end.

Variations on a simple shape

Fir Trees

The individual fir tree pattern shown below repeated and overlapped. Stitched on even-weave linen.

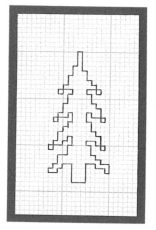

a A design drawn on graph paper.

b Stitched on even-weave cotton.

c Stitched on scrim and mounted on white card which shows through.

d Crosses worked on hessian – the background filled in, the tree left void.

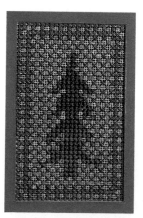

e Canvas sprayed with gold paint and stitched in silks for richness. Medieval chequered effect.

f The design stitched freely on silk.

A morning of drawing proved fruitful. I did a lot of sketches, doodles and little experiments with pen and pencil to see if anything emerged that would be worth developing.

The distorted net effect was discovered by doodling. I crossed some pencil lines in an irregular way, filled the 'boxes' with penned crosses and then rubbed out many of the pencil lines. Not an important discovery but fun to do. Tack the lines, work the crosses and then remove tacking.

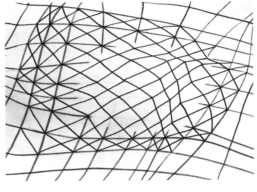

Waves was the most interesting doodle. It came spontaneously and immediately suggested the sea. I transferred the design onto the fabric using the same technique as for the cherry tree. I knew this sketch would lead to further sea embroideries.

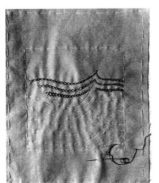

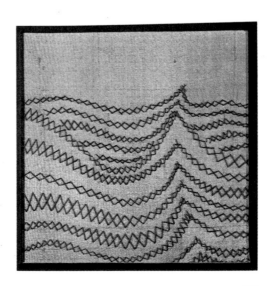

Permission to be free

It is difficult at first – especially if you enjoy traditional cross stitch – to think of it in terms of mood and movement. But crosses can lean and sway, dance all over the fabric or be heavy and strong. Lines of stitches can float and flow or suggest energetic purposeful movement. Crosses can be isolated or tumbled on top of each other. Variation in weight and direction can create any mood.

I stopped feeling uneasy that I was not using cross stitch in the traditional uniform style when I said to myself that two lines can cross each other in a thousand different ways. They can come alive at my bidding; there are no rules to stop me. Actually saying this gave me the freedom to explore the possibilities.

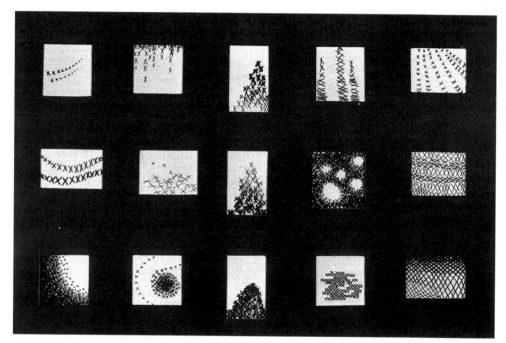

The sheet of experimental stitched sketches shows some effects that can be created. Try some yourself, with thread or pen, to suggest loneliness, lightness, heaviness, strength, conflict, dejection, calm – and movements such as thrusting, falling, floating and fluttering. Closeness of crosses affects the mood a lot.

Two very freely worked scenes. I embroidered on the river bank while my son fished. I worked on calico without any drawing and tried to give an impression of what I saw in the fields. First stitches often look unpromising, so do not give up. The effect improves as you build up layers of texture. (I stitched a little sky first as it is harder to add later.) I am often asked how long work takes and I never know. These two took four hours each and they are 9 cm across.

An experiment with free-flowing lines. Usually I prefer to work on a frame but for this flowing stitching I work in the hand as the needle then goes in and out in one movement – the lines flow and mingle better, creating texture and rhythm. Some of the effects come from varying the size of crosses, some from change of thread. I work stitches from right to left and then turn the work upside down and sew back on the next row. This helps to keep the movement going.

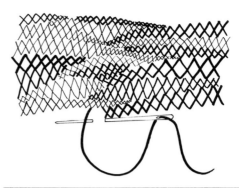

The Cornfield was worked in this flowing method. The size and colour of the stitches varied and some overlapped.

For those still apprehensive about working cross stitch freely, I suggest one subject that you do not have to draw and about which you cannot be stuffy – just make a few rough and irregular stitches and let them take over, have fun: EMBROIDER A SCARECROW.

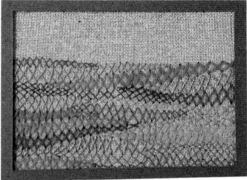

Choose a piece of fabric big enough. Scarecrows always turn out to be 'characters' and they may need a field or other background. A coarse material such as hessian or loosely woven furnishing fabric is suitable as you can stitch on it with wool or other thick thread, make holes in it, withdraw threads from it or fray the edges. If you prefer a small scale, a miniature scarecrow can be stitched with finer materials. Look at the scarecrows on the next two pages.

Scarecrows

Some scarecrows worked in my classes by students who had never embroidered cross stitch freely before.

Kate Rowlands

Edna Hannam

Beryl Willis

Doreen Holt

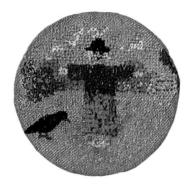

Vera Bradshaw

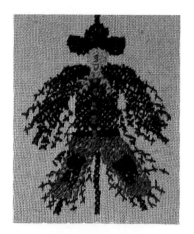

Winifred Herriot

Beppy Berlin

Molly Robinson

Pauline Banon

Sheila Taylor

Joyce Bowles

I. Dann

Y. Wills

June Middleton

Janet Gammer

E. K. Smith

Enid Streets

Some simple ways to begin designing

Draw or trace a simple shape and make it your own. Spend an hour or two with pens, ruler, scissors and tracing paper. Play with your shape. Once you start enjoying the process, more ideas will come. Make a template of your shape and draw several outlines in pencil. Elaborate your shapes with pen and then erase the outline. Such simple design techniques can be seen developed into embroideries throughout this book.

Here are a few simple designs based on the outline of a pear. In case you wonder what has happened to the last pear, the template has been cut up and the pieces arranged to make a pattern.

Pear embroidered. This was worked on fine silk backed with calico. A little pink was painted on the calico to show through the silk where the pear shape is left void. The background to this shape was stitched with single threads of stranded cotton in a variety of pastel shades. The pears on the mount were painted.

Two ways of simplifying that help you design for embroidery

1 Viewfinders

a Make 'window' viewfinders in cardboard. Make several different sizes in both squares and rectangles. They will enable you to limit the areas you see by putting a frame round them – rather like looking through a camera – and they are particularly helpful out of doors in isolating a small part of a large scene. If you are looking at something like a hedgerow, a bed of flowers or dense foliage it can seem overwhelmingly complicated, but isolate a small area and you will begin to visualise it in stitches.

b Make two L-shaped pieces of card. These will provide you with an adjustable 'window' for use on photographs, books, drawings, etc. Move them around to make tall areas, wide areas, areas at a different angle. Put the main focus (such as a face, figure or building) to one side of the 'window' or half out of it and a totally different effect may be created. A small part of a photograph may be more interesting than the whole or may suggest an abstract pattern quite unrelated to the original. Isolating small areas may highlight textures not even noticed before. Such exercises start ideas flowing.

2 Tracing paper

It is invaluable for simplifying designs. Look at a photograph through tracing paper and trace a few simple shapes. Try it several times, varying the strong areas. These tracings can be the basis of a design. Try the following:

a Fill in the background and leave the object void.

b Move the tracings round and place the strong areas differently to make a new design.

c Lay one tracing over another and make a third that is different again.

d Look through the tracing paper for blocks of dark and light – do not draw outlines. Shade in the very dark areas in black, the greys with lines or dots – spacing them out as greys grow lighter, with none at all in the palest areas. When you lift off the tracing, you have simple strong shapes that are a splendid basis for embroidery. Dramatic effects can be obtained if tones are limited to just black and white.

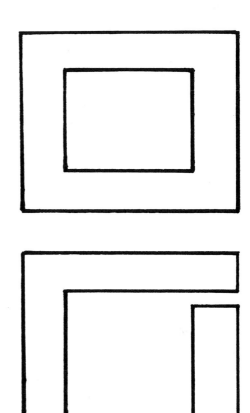

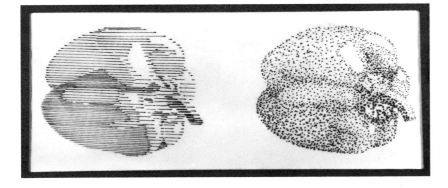

A Capsicum would be hard to draw and even harder to imagine in embroidery. By tracing only the light and dark areas, you immediately have an embroidery design.

Some simple ways to begin designing

A detailed photograph of a building was simplified and slightly altered. Several tracings were made before a suitable design emerged.

Here are three tracings of one man's head. In each the tonal value was the only interest. The first head is in dots, the second is more starkly reduced to black and white and the third is in lines. All these methods are more easily converted into embroidery than outline drawings.

The Jazz Singer was simplified with tracing paper. After several versions I decided to reduce it to black and white to give a stronger impact. I wanted to express a feeling of volume and vigour. The design was finally stitched on evenweave linen.

A newspaper photograph was the starting point for this group of *Arab Women*. The very basic form came from repeated drawing, tracing and collage. Cutting or tearing paper shapes is another way to make detailed designs simple and manageable. When I was satisfied with the group I drew it on squared paper.

The first embroidery was worked on fine canvas with silk thread to give richness and the robes are patterned. The second two are simpler, worked on even-weave linen. The first has the figures embroidered, the second has the figures as voids with the background stitched.

The final version was in free stitching on silk fabric.

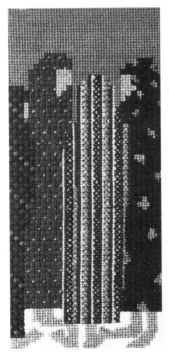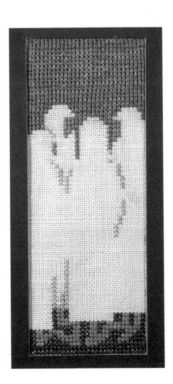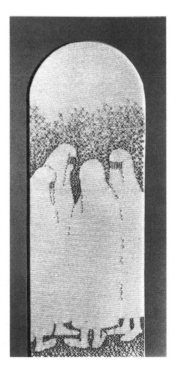

Some simple ways to begin designing

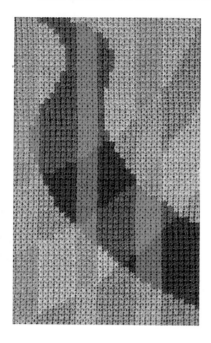

One of the doodles worked out on squared paper and stitched in wool on canvas.

Doodles

Most people doodle unselfconsciously. Just making marks all over a piece of paper can have a spark of creativity in it and can be the start of a design. Confidence comes with a lot of doodling!

The most daunting way to start is to face oneself with a large sheet of white paper (even coloured is a little kinder) so I collect a great pile of scrap: backs of calendars, cards, computer paper, anything that is inexpensive and plentiful so that I can do a dozen doodles on them straight off. I usually draw squares and rectangles of different sizes on the paper first to give a frame to work in but my lines frequently go over the edge of the frame and back again.

I often do my drawings to music! When I have a good pile, I lay them out and choose one or two that seem to work better. Use of L-shaped viewfinders reveals that small parts are sometimes more interesting than the whole. I draw a frame round such areas and enlarge them if necessary. I select one or two that please me and develop them.

As an exercise you can trace out several copies of each and try to fill in areas with different degrees of dark and light using pen or pencil. Then do them again in colour. You may feel that one of them inspires you to embroider it but maybe not – it does not really matter – what is important is that you are starting to design and it is a technique that you improve at.

Here is a sheet of my doodles. The first two are simple doodles, the others are developments of parts of doodles. The last one is a little more designed (lines crossing with some shapes added) but I still worked in the same free way and did lots of them.

Ruled doodles

As an alternative, you can doodle with lines drawn with a ruler. This must be just as free – do not hesitate or plan at all. Draw lines in all directions and as many as you like. Straight lines surround spaces which are geometric in shape and this opens up new ideas for patterns. When you come to develop these drawings you will probably need to rub out or alter some of the lines in order to create larger areas. After that, work in the same way as for the scribbled doodles.

Here is a sheet of geometric designs. The first is a doodle worked out in three tones. The second two consist of paper triangles. (Cut squares in half to make triangles.) When you actually handle them, intriguing arrangements soon develop. The pieces in the triangle-wheel were chosen for their tonal differences. In the centre is one of a series of designs with a circle in a rectangle. I freely ruled overlapping geometric shapes in the rest of the area, the circle remaining the focal point. On the right is the side of a modern glass building – a wonderful design for a piece of embroidery with subtle colour changes.

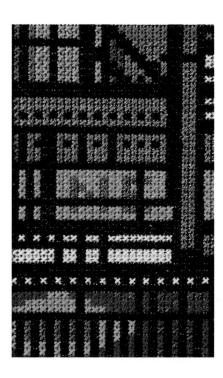

Left: an embroidery based on the circle and geometric shapes.

Right: a piece of canvas work. It is a development of straight lines into something which is semi-pictorial.

Some simple ways to begin designing

Further thoughts on doodles

I was so inspired by Paul Klee's scribbled trees that I tried to do something on these lines, again drawing quite freely and doing it in one line. The main thing I learnt from this exercise was: what a brilliant artist! – it looks so easy and it isn't!

The two embroidered trees came from different drawings. In both cases the designs were drawn onto tissue paper and the sewing lines tacked onto the fabric as for the cherry tree (page 13).

1 The more formal interpretation worked on even-weave fabric with regular crosses.

2 A freely stitched version on patterned furnishing fabric. As it was an experimental piece I made myself use the patterned material – now I think it is more interesting than plain calico.

Colour magazines

Much embroidery is best designed with cut or torn paper and a lot of professionals work in this way. It helps to assess tone, colour and shape. Colour magazines are a designer's best friend. There is a wonderful choice of colours and the black and white pages enable you to work with tones ranging from white through the greys to black. Just the variations in the print make subtle differences of tone. Pieces can be moved around or replaced and you can take a good look at the background area which is called the negative shape. Torn paper can be built up in layers to create faces, figures, scenes, animals, etc.

Sometimes it is more effective to repeat one shape than to change the shape. Perhaps the most rewarding of all is to cut out geometric shapes and to build up patterns. The advantage that sticking paper has over painting (apart from being less inhibiting) is that you can keep altering the design until you are satisfied with the arrangement.

It is very helpful to prop up a design where it can be seen frequently. Peer at it through half-closed eyes. Turn it upside down and sideways – the balance should be pleasing all ways. Look at it in a mirror as this can show up faults. When you finally feel that it is right, stick it down and view it through your L-shaped viewfinder. You may want to move the focal point more to one side, to bring the frame in and compress the subject or to make it a different shape. It may save stitching time to consider these points at an early stage, but you will have to assess your embroidery continually until it is finished.

Kelly's Bar started as a very gluey mixture of cut and torn paper. The result excited me enough to embroider it. The drawn detail on right shows more of the inside. (See embroidery on page 49.)

Roofs of Florence was designed in cut paper. I wanted to suggest the brightness of the Italian sun and hard shadows. I made the buildings in squares and rectangles to reinforce the hard outlines created by the light. I continued the squares into the blue sky. (See page 41.)

Getting to know a subject: Poppies

There is real understanding of a subject only when it has been drawn, designed and embroidered in several different ways. Sadly there is not the time to do this with every subject but try it sometimes. Study a small piece of garden or a tree throughout one year. Move around with your eyes open, make notes on the back of bus tickets if need be, make scribble sketches, photograph tiny interesting areas as well as grand scenes. Collect cuttings and reproductions. Specialise in one or two themes for a while and keep all this information in a folder or scrapbook. You may not embroider it for years but I guarantee that it will prove a most useful source of reference – and that it will make you observe in a more creative way.

Poppies are so fragile and transitory that I felt it a challenge to capture their delicacy. I painted them several times but they looked heavy next to the flowers. A collage made with red tissue paper and green wool came nearest to suggesting them.

My first embroidery of poppies was drawn on squared paper and worked on even-weave material in traditional regular cross stitch.

I worked on poppies for some time, long after the flowers had dropped. As always, when embroidering any subject, I pinned on a board all the pictures I could find. This, together with my own sketches and photographs, keeps my ideas fresh and mobile.

For free poppies I embroidered directly onto the fabric with no preparation apart from studying poppies. Beginning is a daunting moment: you thread up the needle and make the first cross in space! But have courage, try a few quick sketches and one will come alive.

For *the cornfield with poppies* I lightly painted the material, rough cotton, a golden yellow. I painted it rather than using a yellow fabric because I like the uneven effect. Eager to start I nearly began stitching the poppies but realised that I would get a much freer movement if I did the corn first. I worked deeper yellow crosses in the front, gradually using smaller paler stitches towards the horizon.

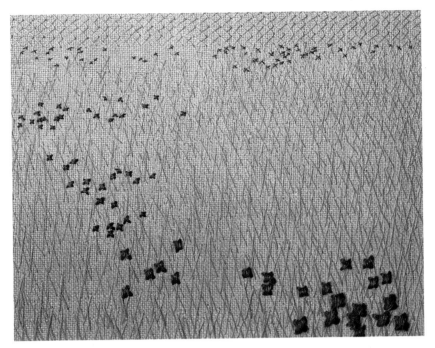

Backgrounds are often painted with the ground one colour and the sky another but in this embroidery I wanted the whole to be yellow, to give the feeling of a hazy golden glow throughout. I just added some regular blue stitches to indicate sky.

It is interesting to experiment with painting backgrounds – try two or three different colours for the same scene. If the cornfield background had been painted blue, the feel would be quite different – it would suggest another time of day or a colder day. Large areas of grey sky can make a stronger impact than red poppies. So think about the mood created by the background fabric or colour even before you add a stitch!

The three card designs show an impression of poppies painted on silk with some stitches added. It is quite remarkable how a little sketch which looks quite flat sparks into life with the addition of threads. This is a relatively quick way to achieve an attractive design and is suitable for cards, calendars and little gifts. There is more information about painting on silk and other fabrics on page 46.

Colours

What excitement and frustration they cause – they have a life of their own. They shift about in a totally independent way, but they are the essence of life and create the mood of all our work.

Embroidering countryside scenes in soft browns and greens, or seas and skies in blue, are safe and usually attractive but I beg you not to stick there. Have a go at working strong or unusual combinations of colours. It is not always easy but it is challenging and rewarding.

Choose the brightest colours and they may turn up their toes and die on you; choose gentle colours and bid them be quiet and they suddenly start quarrelling and one takes over. Hardest of all, you can choose a beautiful coloured thread, say blue, to stitch with and before you have so much as drunk a cup of coffee, he will have snuggled up to his friends and will grin up at you looking green or mauve! Do not be frightened of using new colour schemes and discovering how colours work – even through a few exercises you will learn to appreciate their interaction. Some people may then go back to working in more familiar colours but trying some adventurous and exciting combinations will make you more aware of colours in everyday life and more appreciative of the skill of artists and craftsmen who use them.

Collect reproductions wherever you go and study them. Look at the blocks of colour that Klee uses. Kandinsky and Delauney combine wonderful circles and shapes in colours that spin and move. Bridget Riley makes colours move in a quite different way and because they work so well they look simple.

I urge everyone to try some abstract designs or patterns or bold pictures cut out in coloured paper.

Tone

As important as colour, tone is the amount of light and dark and the balance of light and dark is one of the main qualities that gives a work interest and life. You can judge it best by looking through half-closed eyes or by imagining the subject photographed in black and white. You will immediately appreciate the importance of tonal weight. A piece of work in beautiful colours that are the same 'weight' will be flat and dull, though probably all it needs is the addition of some lighter and darker areas. They can be of the same colours that you have chosen, but paler or darker in tone.

Anyone interested in studying colour and tone should read *Embroidery and Colour* by Constance Howard.

Four colour exercises

My aim was to stitch a series of exercises, not choosing colours that I particularly liked but less familiar schemes to see how they worked out. The results varied in their success.

1 Yellow is one of the strongest colours to use. I worked rows of brilliant yellow thread in different textures and added some touches of bright blue to see if it could hold its own.

2 This piece breaks all the rules: strong colours used in more or less equal quantities, jangling around, bumping into each other, not much difference in their tonal weight. But the black outlines overcame this problem. One would not choose it for bedroom wallpaper but it is vigorous. No colour has any particular impact because of the fragmentation. It was quite roughly stitched in wool at different angles.

3 In this exercise I wanted to use a family of colours, in this case pinky browns, with each block of colour outlined in the complementary colour. I looked through my scrapbooks to get inspiration for some shapes to fill in and I saw a photograph of railway lines.

4 The aim of this exercise was to work in another family of colours and to make the whole as rich as possible. I chose blue ranging from mauve to blue-green, with a background of bright turquoise. All the coloured threads heaped on a tray were strong and brilliant; you would not have believed that they could ever seem dull. I knew that I was disregarding tone when I first stitched but I was sure that this mixture would stay bright. I was wrong, it fell as flat as a pancake, but I managed to lift it with some pale and dark threads.

This piece of work, more than any other I have done, showed the total change in the appearances of a colour when laid next to another. There is no colour in it warmer than mauve and yet it looks pink; on the other side, greens that look quite grassy are in fact blue-green. I added one green that had a little more yellow in it but had to remove it as it stood out as brown! The choice of mount also played an important part. I tried several colours but the dark mauve had the most dramatic effect. The whole appearance is quite rich but the turquoise rather than the colour of the threads dominates.

Colours

A new colour scheme

It is often difficult to create a new colour scheme out of the air or to work a conventional subject in unconventional colours. One way is to choose a picture in which the colours excite you and for preference not a picture normally related to your subject. Then search through magazines for the exact colours in your pictures. Cut out blocks of these colours, ignoring shape, but in the same proportions as they are used by the artist. This soon makes you appreciate that orange, for example, is no longer just orange but a colour that varies in a hundred ways from yellow to red, and in as many tones. Do this exercise with cut paper, carefully finding every colour as accurately as you can and stick it down. Put your picture away so that the subject does not distract you and take a fresh look at your design with an entirely new colour scheme.

Little Houses – I wanted to do a bright interpretation of stylised houses and chose to work it in the colours of Paul Klee's *Little Face*, so did the exercise with cut paper. I planned to use coton à broder on canvas and soon realised that with such a range of oranges this was a job for the dye pot. I had a great morning brewing up colours, often putting a variety of different coloured threads in one dye so that they emerged with a lovely related look. The result is seen in a colourful heap. I knew by the nature of the design and the similarity of the colours that I had to pay great attention to the tonal value. From constantly watching this throughout my stitching, I got the idea for a further development.

I simplified the design of my houses to an architectural pattern which could be viewed all four ways, and stitched it in tones of brown.

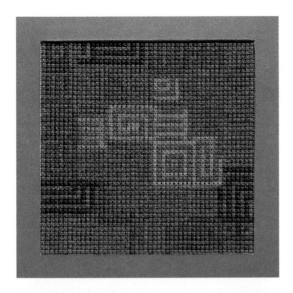

Two experiments in yellow

Lines in Ochre – This is a piece of work for which I did a lot of preparation. The geometric pattern was drawn on graph paper and painted up in a variety of colours. I had them propped around me for a while; the large focal area was sometimes light and sometimes dark. I finally chose to embroider in heavy yellow ochre against a range of turquoise blue.

Radiating Yellow – This is a large embroidery inspired by the words of Kandinsky and worked with enthusiasm and no preparation. Kandinsky wrote:

> Yellow is a warm colour, it moves towards the spectator, it radiates outwards in an eccentric way, this increases with the lighter shades, there is no such thing as deep very dark yellow – yellow has properties of material energy which it pours out unconsciously over an aspect and diffuses aimlessly in all directions.

I decided to embroider a burst of yellow – thousands of yellow stitches radiating outwards. I started to stitch on a piece of irregularly dyed fabric but it proved to be too small – I had got carried away – so I mounted that on a piece of aubergine furnishing fabric, a little of which colour is in the centre amidst the blue.

Many stitches later when my energy, if not the energy in the yellow, finally petered out, I mounted the work and felt it needed a border but not a break in the colour. So I made a frame and dyed the wood the same aubergine as the mount.

33

Faces

Can a face be embroidered in cross stitch, I wondered . . . This black and white portrait was my first attempt. I simplified a photograph by using tracing paper – in this case, a colour photograph which can be difficult to visualise in black and white. However, tracing paper blurs out a lot of the colour and peering through half-closed eyes helps to pick out the various tones from dark to light and to block them in accordingly. When I had a satisfactory tracing, I laid 'graph' tracing paper over it and retraced, squaring up the tonal areas. You can buy tracing paper with graph paper lines printed on it or you can rule your own lines on tracing paper.

Now the design was ready for embroidery on an open-weave fabric whose threads I could count. I used an even-weave linen and used different thicknesses of thread to create a varying density.

My two ladies with hats were among my earliest attempts at working faces in free cross stitch. Both designs were drawn, then traced onto tissue paper and tacked onto the fabric. As always, I had my original drawings and photographs at my side for reference as I stitched. I have made scrapbooks for years and now have a shelf of them and keep adding! I use them constantly for they are a great source of ideas and reference. Some pictures I like less as time goes by and others more.

My elderly **Lady from Provence** with the deep striking eyes and strong mouth was always compelling. I had two small photographs to work from and when I decided to embroider her the face had to be enlarged considerably. I drew it many times until I really knew her. To get a faint hint of colouring I sprayed calico with weak dye, stretched muslin over it and stitched through both layers.

Christina was also worked on a close-weave fabric. Here I wanted to put the barest minimum of stitches on the face to keep it delicate and to make the hat and scarf thick and cosy.

Old Woman's Face – Denim is a fabric that I have explored a lot as it has so many possibilities. There is a striking difference in tone from one side of the fabric to the other and there is the bonus that you can sew with unravelled threads, gaining darker and lighter tones from the fabric itself. When I wanted to do a strong rugged face, it seemed just right to use denim for the background material to stitch crosses with unravelled threads.

Japanese Ladies – the three heads were taken from different sources so the design element came from simplification and in the combination of the three into one pattern.

If you have children's paintings available you never need be short of inspiration! *James* was a joint effort: James aged four was the painter and I was the stitcher. He was covering my kitchen walls with lovely paintings, all bursting with life and colour. I suddenly had the idea of embroidering one. We had great fun routing through bags of wool and chose colours together. James said, 'Red is our flavourite colour.'

(Faces: see also page 22 for the Jazz Singer.)

Figures

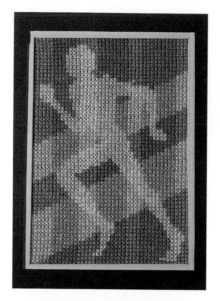

Figure of a **Runner** designed as a pattern and stitched on canvas.

Nude Figure – so far my only attempt. I started using large stitches and she looked hairy so now I have worked it in small ones and she looks like a bad case of measles. I am sure it can be done. One day I will try again!

Little Musician – developed from a minute figure, one of many musicians on an illuminated manuscript of AD 1250–60.

The fine canvas on which it was worked was first sprayed with Christmas gold paint. For richness, I stitched in silk and built up a wide patterned border to echo the decorations on a manuscript.

Woolly Girls on Calico – I indulged my liking for sturdy little girls in a series of sketches. I stitched two of them. They were jolly to do and show what a good 'filling' stitch cross stitch can be.

After a wonderful holiday in New Zealand I came home with my head full of ideas and longing to embroider everything from Maori designs, mountain scenery and the Bush, to Windy Wellington. I did not know where to begin! So I drew and drew, lots of quick sketches to hold the ideas while I was getting back to household routine. I jotted down word pictures, too, and colour schemes. I did some torn paper impressions and, of course, I had photographs. After a month I felt quite relaxed, ideas became clearer. As they were recorded in some way, albeit roughly, there was no rush to begin stitching. Since that holiday I have used the ideas that I had collected in many different ways.

On the left is my paper collage of **Windy Wellington**.
On the right is my embroidery. It was a sturdy design and I felt that to work it on denim with unravelled thread was right. I did not include the tree; it could possibly provide reference for another embroidery. The pale side of the denim is used for the picture and the dark side for the mount.

Trees

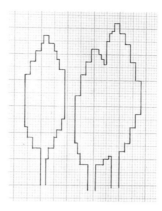

Poplar Trees – one of my early pieces of cross stitch. It was worked on even-weave linen, the crosses are all the same size but are scattered freely and are in varying tones of grey. A silhouette of the trees was worked out on squared paper and the basic shapes were left void. It was the last time that I designed a tree on squared paper – it leaves so little room for development in the course of stitching.

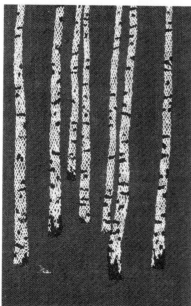

Trunks of Silver Birch – the first study is on silk and the second on denim, stitched with the unravelled threads of the fabric.

Little Copse – I drove past as a brilliant sun shone through the trees. The grass and the trees made straight bands against the yellow. I stopped and drew it. I knew I had a piece of yellow material just the right colour so I rushed home and went through my drawers as a dog digs up a bone! I overlaid, twisted and ruched transparent fabrics to get the effect of the trees and the grass. Then I held them lightly in place with cross stitch. I did it quickly just to capture the scene.

Fir Tree in Mist – this was inspired by a visit to the Great Japan exhibition. I was thrilled by the wonderful use of space and liked the gold-leaf squares that backed a lot of the paintings. But I set myself a lot of problems when I tried to work very pale squares of blue and green in a similar way. I had a great range of threads laid out on a tray and they all looked quite compatible but when I began to stitch in blocks it was quite unbelievable how some colours jumped out and others merged and became indistinguishable. I did a lot of unpicking before I achieved the effect I wanted.

My Tree in Summer – There is a field near my home which I have photographed over three years in different seasons and lights. The large picture was the first embroidery, worked freely on a loosely-woven cotton. The tree trunk shows the Impressionist influence and was stitched in every conceivable colour from soot, blue, green, dull red, mauve and grey, to ochre – all the colours you see if you peer closely at the trunk of a tree. The poppies were stitched with thin strips of nylon fabric – this is very useful for sewing as it does not break and creates a nice bulky effect.

The other versions were more experimental. The first was in the colours of Monet's paintings, embroidered with silk threads on shot silk. The mount was of the same material. The second version was on calico and entirely stitched in thick wool and finer threads in varying shades of white. The third picture was on scrim. Some areas such as the fence, sky and field were left empty. Scrim being so loosely woven, it can be mounted over any colour and this shows through. Scrim is a good material to work on but care must be taken to leave no loose ends at the back. They must be darned in or they show when the scrim is mounted.

Buildings

Elizabethan Knot Garden and House – it seemed right to work this formal house and garden in a traditional way – regular cross stitch on even-weave linen. I did some research and found that the Elizabethans liked views through arches and tunnels. So I contrived a frame of a balustrade with miniature tree and branches overhanging the sides and top. This frame is in wool and of quite strong colours whereas the house and garden within are paler in finer thread.

Later I worked two urban scenes in contrasting styles but as a pair; one quite 'modern' design in conventional cross stitch and the other freely on silk.

Skyscraper – this was planned on graph paper and stitched on fine canvas. It was very enjoyable to do as the method suited the subject.

Gas-holder – this was worked freely which enabled me to stitch the reflection as I wanted. The only thing I had to be exact about was the structure of the gasholder. I drew it out, traced it onto tissue paper and tacked it very accurately onto the silk. The rest I stitched quite freely from the drawing by my side.

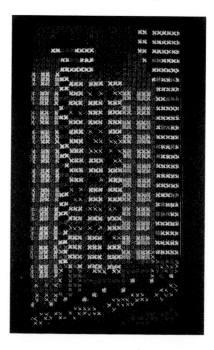

40

Factory Chimneys – this was a fantasy piece which I wanted to be fun, a mixture of the chimneys which I love, and a country scene. There is quite a lot of glitter and gold thread in it and the billowing smoke shows the white watered silk on which the picture is worked. I thought a bright yellow sky would be startling but the more dotty one gets the more normal it looks!

Here are impressions from two holidays. As well as the scenes, I wanted to capture the different qualities of light. The scene on the left is in Italy and the one on the right in Cornwall.

I described on page 27 how *Roofs of Florence* was designed in cut paper. Many of the threads were dyed and those in the shadows briefly plunged in a black dye. For *Cornish Village* – so much in contrast to the bright sun and hard shadows of Italy – I wanted everything diffused in the soft light of the West Country. I dyed the background material a pale grey-blue and plunged all my threads for a moment or two in the same dye. I felt it appropriate to stitch the two pictures differently in order to emphasise their contrasting qualities.

Scenes

All these pictures are embroidered in free cross stitch.

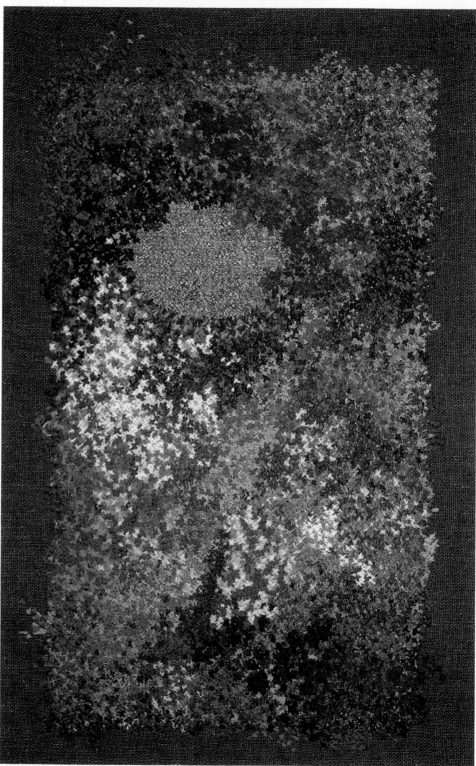

Overgrown Garden – a large hanging which is very much textured with stitches built up to several layers in places. It is worked mostly in wool but it has a few shiny threads to lift it. (See also page 6.)

Harwell amidst the Cornfields

Waterfall – stitched on furnishing fabric. To get a range of colours in the rocks I often worked with two or three different colours of stranded thread or fine wool in the needle at once. The water is in shiny man-made thread and the foam at the bottom is loosely stitched in fluffy wool.

Cornish Clay Pits – the wonderful 'moon' landscapes created by the workings near St Austell could keep me embroidering for years. On bright days the water in the pits takes on the most brilliant colours and the white is dazzling; at night they are just as dramatic.

I chose a very smooth, very white poly-cotton to work on because I did not want to stitch the clay – it is so pure it had to be left void.

Widening horizons

Dyeing

I began by doing a little dyeing for special pieces of work but, like many embroiderers, I now dye a great deal. One advantage is that by mixing colours myself I get a much greater range of subtle shades not found in bought fabrics and threads. Since I have been doing my own dyeing I find that I do not like the flatness of many commercially dyed fabrics and there are a lot of very boring materials that look a lot better for a dip – it can bring them alive. Do not stick to dyeing white fabrics and threads – far from it. Coloured materials yield up some gorgeous and unpredictable results.

With threads it is particularly successful to process as follows: dye one batch in the basic colour; as long as there is some 'body' left in the dye, add a small quantity of a different colour before dyeing the next batch; repeat this several times and you will end up with a lovely subtle range of colours.

There is a variety of dyes on the market which are very satisfactory, Dylon being the most easily available on the UK market. Select the right kind of dye – there is one for natural materials and one for synthetics. Follow the instructions and it is a very simple process. New materials need to be washed thoroughly before being dyed so that all dressing is removed. Some words of caution: firstly, the colour ends up paler when the fabrics have been thoroughly rinsed and dried than they appear in the dye but the colour can be made deeper by storing the materials in a plastic bag immediately they come out of the dye, and leaving for a few hours in a warm place before rinsing. Secondly, one usually makes up far too much dye at the beginning and, faced with a large quantity of a lovely colour, there is a mad tendency to fling in curtains, blouses and shirts and to end up in desperation dyeing the cat's blanket! One rarely needs a whole tin of dye, so one either has to gauge smaller quantities or mix the contents of a tin of dye into a half pint solution and store it in a bottle to use as required. Add the 'fixer' only to the quantity you are about to use, because once it has been added, the solution will remain active for only a few hours. Experimenting with mixing colours can yield some stunning results – it is a process one has to try for oneself.

Summer – all the materials and threads were dyed, some specifically for this piece but one or two strips and all the pinks and reds came from my 'dye bag'.

I keep all my painted and dyed fabrics, even very small pieces if they are of unusual colour. They are invaluable. If you need a colour to 'lift' some work you can try out a dozen combinations from the dye bag. If you cannot instantly feel how to express something that has inspired you, make a fabric collage and let it germinate for a bit. Materials from the dye bag can spark off unusual colour schemes and the sight of all the beautiful colours jumbled up as you tip them out is much more exciting than a pile of new folded fabrics. What is even more important, you are not reluctant to tear, twist and enjoy trying them out – after all, you created them!

Dyeing and painting fabric

Dyeing and painting fabric

In recent years there has been a great development in painting on fabric by various methods. But if you study the history of embroidery you will see that it has been done for centuries! There are several excellent fabric paints on the market that make it easier.

The painting can be very simple: from just colouring the background with one or two washes or adding a little more detail such as skyline, trees, paths, etc., to detailed painting (this may require a thickener to prevent running). A little colouring is certainly a more encouraging starting point than a blank piece of material. If you have not tried painting on fabric before, stretch some material, mix two or three saucers of colour and try painting with large and small pieces of plastic sponge. This can yield up some lovely impressions if you practise a bit (see Rosemary's Notebook, page 64). If you prefer, try painting with a sponge on paper first. If you decide to use a brush, make it a large one so that you do not get too detailed. Add a few stitches and you will get some lively results.

Red Arrows – John, who fished at fifteen and played the guitar at sixteen (see page 51) was later in the University Air Squadron and needed something to decorate his college walls. An embroidery of the Red Arrows seemed appropriate but depicting smoke in cross stitch was perhaps pushing the boundaries of credibility a bit far. However, the picture does show how the fields were painted.

Tall House – this house in a square in London's Mayfair really is as tall and narrow as this – I stood in the street and drew it and, to be sure, I photographed it! I painted the house on heavy cotton and my aim was to make it dark at the bottom, with this part heavily embroidered, and paler towards the top in order to increase the effect of height, with painting and stitching both growing paler. If I were doing a building again and wanted to grade the colour, I would spray it. It would have meant a lot of masking of areas to be left unpainted but would have been more satisfactory.

Painting on silk – use fine or medium smooth silk. It should be washed first to remove dressing and then stretched tightly on a frame (best secured with masking tape as pins can pull a thread). The traditional technique is with gutta percha outlining areas of the design to be dyed. These lines must join and penetrate the silk or the colours will bleed.

For a less controlled look, dyes can be applied without gutta outlines or can be slightly checked by water soluble ink outlines and a quick blow with a hair drier.

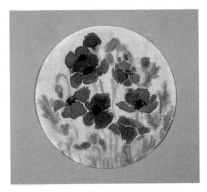

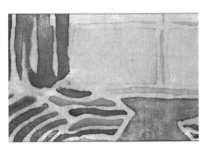

Poppies – painting on silk with water soluble ink. Outline did not hold the dye in one area at the top – hence one extra poppy!

Window – painting on silk with gutta percha outlining.

Transfer paints – these are painted onto paper and then ironed onto the fabric. I used them for the two portraits of John on page 51. As you need to end up with the design on the fabric the same way round as the original painting, try the method that I use. I trace my design onto greaseproof paper. Then I turn it over and lay it on white paper so that the outline shows through. I paint the design with fabric paints (at this point it is in reverse) and when it is quite dry, I turn it over again and iron the design onto the fabric – the right way round, an exact impression and several prints can be taken.

Crayons – there are fabric crayons to use directly onto the material and to fix by ironing; others to use on paper and to iron onto the fabric. The effect with both is bold but the colours are rather crude. The sea was a second print from a drawing on paper.

Spraying – another way of colouring fabric which gives a different effect from painting. The gradation of colours is attractive and the masking of certain areas can make a strong impact. Spray diffusers come in a variety of prices and sophistication and work very well though the technique needs some practice. This is a piece of fabric sprayed with a Humbrol Air Brush – and similar to the one used in the Sea embroidery (page 71).

Painting on calico – the first tree was painted with watercolour paints on un-washed calico, the second on washed calico where colours blur much more.

Summer Field – painted on canvas. The sky is left just painted and the stitching comes in finely and intermittently in the distant fields. Further towards the front of the picture, the stitching takes over and in the foreground the threads are very thick and textured.

Clifftops – the design was drawn with fibre tip pens. I like taking photographs at ground level so that I can view scenes through grass, flowers or rocks. I find that this adapts well to embroidery.

'Vilene under a veil'

If you remain not too happy about painting, try this quick project. You need thick Vilene, a simple picture or photograph with some interest in the foreground, a selection of colouring materials (paints, felt and fibre tip pens, crayons, soft black pencil . . .) and some muslin or other transparent material (thin nylon scarves are ideal). Also some embroidery threads. Draw and colour your picture on the Vilene with a mixture of media if you wish. If you paint, use a dryish brush for detail and for large areas have a piece of soft paper ready to blot the colour – this presses the colour into the Vilene and gives quite a good effect. When the picture is dry, lay the transparent fabric over the picture. Try unusual colours, such as pink nylon over a landscape. This gives a glowing effect where black muslin makes it look like night. Tack down the fabric and add stitches in foreground.

Snow in Leicestershire – this scene was painted onto Vilene.

Kelly's Bar – this design was created very freely in cut and torn paper (see page 27). It was worked in traditional cross stitch on even-weave fabrics. The unusual feature is that it is on two scales. The outside of the bar is in large stitches on binca and this part was plotted out on graph paper. It was sewn in wool with a few finer threads and Raffene (synthetic raffia) to give a shine in places. Before the red surrounds of the doorway were embroidered, fine canvas was tacked on, the edges of it hidden in large wool crosses. The canvas had a faint impression of the figures painted on it. On this area I used a sharp needle to go through both the canvas and the binca.

Developing ideas

A detail showing the change of scale between the binca and the canvas.

Developing ideas

Impressionist painting

I love the painting of the Impressionists with their vibrating colours and radiant light effects – they make me tingle. I was reading Monet's colour theories at the same time that I was getting excited about crosses – and suddenly realised that a single stitch could be used in the same way as a dot of paint.

I decided to try out this idea by copying as exactly as I could small pieces from paintings by Sisley, Monet and Seurat and this first card of little samples worked well enough to encourage me to go ahead.

It was said of Monet's working method in 1888 that, 'One of his great points is to use the same colours on every part of the canvas. Thus the sky would be slashed with strokes of blue, lake green and yellow, with a preponderance of blue; a green field would work in the same way with a preponderance of green; while a piece of rock would be treated in the same way with a preponderance of red. By working in this way, the same colour appearing all over the canvas, the subtle harmony of nature is successfully obtained without the loss of colour.'

I had done some drawings of my son with the idea that I would embroider them one day and they seemed ideal for this experiment. I wanted to get the colour effects of outdoors and indoors.

Throughout work on these two portraits, I tried to use colour in the way Monet did. And I was influenced by Seurat who eventually abandoned all earth colours from his palette in favour of clear bright ones, the shadows often dotted with the complementary colour. I disciplined myself to using only primary and secondary colours, oversewing quite a lot.

As I wanted the portraits of John to be very close to my original painting, I traced them and used transfer paints, the process described on page 47. In this case I used the paint much diluted as I needed only a faint impression for guidance, not as part of the final work. The first picture is the original painting of John in watercolour and the second is the version in transfer paints, in reverse at this stage.

These portraits are worked in traditional cross stitch on even-weave linen. This led me into a few problems when I started off full of enthusiasm, putting my Impressionist crosses all over the place. I forgot to count the threads to ensure that the crosses would eventually link up – a little unpicking brought me down to earth!

John at fifteen

John at sixteen

Face Emerging – this was inspired by a Russian painting. I walked into a gallery and in one picture a face began to look out from a lot of small patterns in a most subtle way. Exhibitions can often inspire me like this and I rush back home exploding with ideas and beaver away.

Thinking about this picture all the way home, I decided to make a face emerge softly from small pieces of silk. There is a lot of stitching in this embroidery which blends the fragments of fabric.

On another occasion I was inspired by Cubist paintings to embroider a face in the style. I particularly wanted the distortions and angles to add to the understanding of the person and not to caricature.

Man's Head – I made several sketches of a head in an angular style. I chose one to develop and I stylised it, emphasising the planes of the face. I made some tracings at this stage and painted several in an attempt to work out tonal values. This proved to be the hardest thing to get right. When I was satisfied I traced it onto graph paper. Before beginning to stitch the portrait itself I stitched squares of various tones of grey thread to match up with the tonal painting.

When I finished this piece of work I felt pleased. I thought that the face expressed more of the character of the person than a lot of photographs.

Developing ideas

Prisoners of Conscience – There are said to be at least 100,000 prisoners of conscience in the world, imprisoned without trial. Some years ago I had been struggling with the idea of expressing the agony of prisoners and their families (for whom the disappearance of loved ones must be intolerable) in an embroidery. It was events in Chile and the embroideries worked by the women to draw world attention to their plight that inspired me. I felt strongly but I could not find a way of expressing it. Then one day, looking through a Sunday newspaper colour supplement, I saw a picture: the impression made by the hands of Indian women who had pressed them into soft plaster before throwing themselves onto the funeral pyres of their husbands. It was poignant and gave me the idea I wanted. I embroidered a large wall hanging showing the life-sized hands of many men and women. It was worked in a variety of techniques and hangs in the church of All Hallows-by-the-Tower in the City of London.

Here I show *a single hand*, life size and embroidered in cross stitch.

I have recently worked on the same theme again. The representation of *Prisoners disappearing into a black tunnel* is embroidered entirely in cross stitch, which proves itself malleable enough to express every emotion. This time I exploited the ugliness and pain. Many of these prisoners will never emerge – we must not forget them.

Designs for stained glass in paint and cut paper

Another Line of Washing – washing blowing in the wind is such a good subject that it had to be tackled again. The design is livelier than my first effort, shown on page 8. I worked it in the same regular cross stitch on even-weave fabric to remind myself that traditional cross stitch can move and dance as well as free stitching if the design is vigorous.

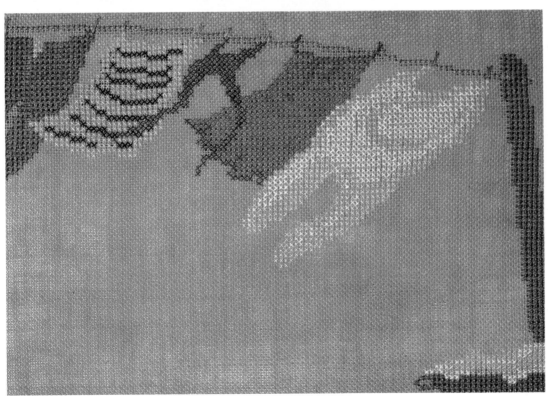

Three-dimensional Sweets. After Vera Bradshaw had embroidered her scarecrow, she went home and produced these amazing sweets.

Mistletoe

Quilted Scene – this little scene was in cross stitch – just to see if it worked!

Fairground – this design was developed straight from doodles. I wanted to embroider an abstract of circles: bright, tight, hard circles and I thought of them constantly as a fairground with spinning wheels, the crowdedness, the glitter and the colour. If you can sense the noise, too, I shall be happy!

I drew up a page of square boxes and doodled circles in all of them. Then I cut them up and restuck them as a collage until I had a design.

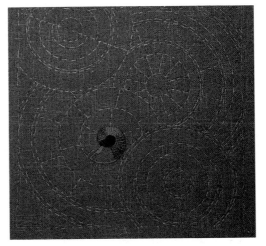

A drawing made from the collage.

The design painted.

The embroidery design – as the circles needed to be very accurate I traced and tacked the design onto fabric in great detail.

The embroidery complete – it is worked in free stitching in a variety of threads and some cords of gold. I gave a lot of thought to the choice of frame. I did not want a mount to diffuse the intensity and I chose a wide, plain, dull gold frame to hold in the spinning wheels.

Experimenting with fabrics

This means shaking yourself out of the traditional and accepted ways of working. Give yourself the freedom to try the unconventional and to make mistakes. Get in the habit of looking at your fabrics and threads in a creative way. As my father used to say, 'There's more than one way to skin a cat!' or, as Edward de Bono puts it more elegantly, 'Lateral thinking'. It requires energy and a sense of fun to experiment but it is rewarding once you get used to it. A lot of ideas will not work as you hope but that does not mean they are failures. So often they are the jumping-off point for the next work.

The pages that follow are my own 'first stage' experiments and I will work on some of them further. They are simple ideas that may encourage embroiderers who have not tried working in this way. Company is stimulating. Join a lively class or gather up a few friends (even one is good) and have a regular day for working together. It is good to share ideas, materials, etc. and to inspire each other.

Striped materials
I decided to embroider my old friend *the runner*. He has, in his day, been silhouetted, repeated, cut up, re-assembled and generally mutilated. Now he was to appear on striped material. I hoped the lines would give a shimmering effect with a faint echo of a shadow figure to suggest movement.

Ridged materials

To stitch between the ridges of fabric with crosses you have to find well-spaced bands. Corded silk or rayon is ideal. Some curtain materials are corded and you can dye them – but allow for shrinkage.

The Jug – I worked out a simple design to give the corded fabric maximum effect and used it diagonally. However, this embroidery involved a great amount of stitching which was not justified by the result. It was a question of scale; the work was too large in relation to the stripes so they did not have sufficient impact. I worked out a sample beforehand, which looked promising but it was much smaller.

Abstracts – two designs on corded rayon stitched with silk. The circular embroidery is mounted in the same material.

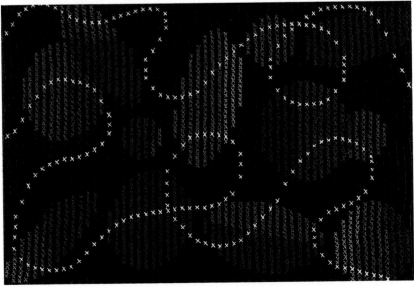

59

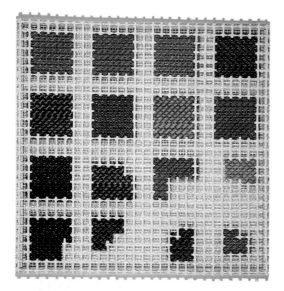

Canvas

We often treat canvas as a base to be covered up at all costs but it is really a very attractive material and one should think of letting it show. Try incorporating the squares as part of a design, colouring it, using different scales or seeing through it.

Canvas colour and mesh size – In this experiment I had two interests: the first was to see the interaction of red and green coloured squares; the second was to use two layers of canvas of different mesh size.

The top layer is rug canvas. To give it a good coating, to stiffen it and to obliterate the dark thread, I applied three layers of white household paint.

Each block of colour was stitched with a shiny thread and with wool and these were changed over. Sometims they just blended without showing, in others they made strong diagonals. In fact each square took on its own personality and degree of dominance. I mounted the work with a thin strip of card between the layers at the edges in order to create some shadow. Looking through one layer of canvas to another could be developed with both patterns and scenes.

Vesuvius – This was worked on rug canvas that had been painted with Dylon Color-fun. Some fine canvas was tacked onto the back at the top of the picture to enable me to do some fine stitching in white at the beginning of the eruption. The surplus fine canvas was then cut away. The rest of the lava was stitched with strips of material, wool of all thicknesses, silk and Raffene (synthetic raffia) for shine. When I had finished stitching the lava, I ruched layers of fine glittering fabrics behind the canvas, pulling it through the holes in places. This was held with a few stitches and glue. For a supply of shiny and often very beautiful transparent materials I would suggest trying to find a shop that supplies stage costumiers – it will have a totally different range of fabrics from a department store. At the end of the book there is the address of a wonderful shop in London – it is like an Aladdin's cave!

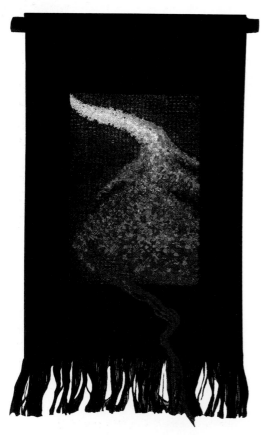

Bulb Field – free cross stitch on fabric, with canvas used as a mount. Fabric and canvas sprayed with green car paint.

Plasterer's scrim – another interesting material. It is very open and loose and comes in medium and coarse weave. It is floppy and unmanageable but looks attractive. I tried painting it with a coat of PVA to retain the natural colour. I also painted it with a thick coat of Dylon Color-fun paint – the scrim absorbed colours in a pleasing way. Both methods stiffened well. Scrim will take aerosol paint but does not stiffen unless previously glued. You can certainly achieve an attractive base to work on.

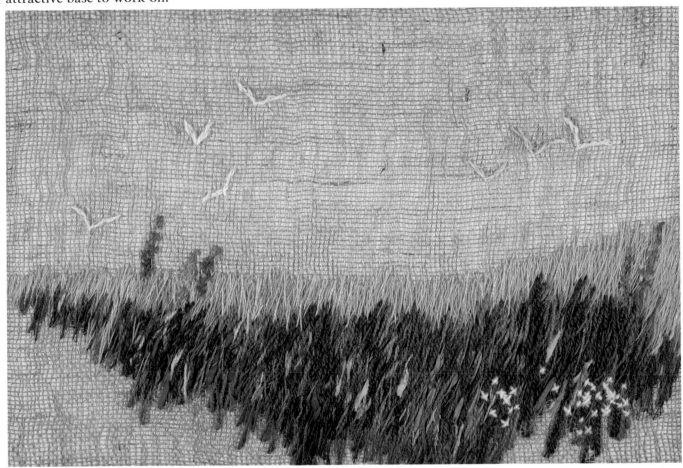

Seagulls over a Cornfield – easily stitched with thick threads and strips of material on stiffened scrim. The colour of the backing can make an interesting difference to the appearance.

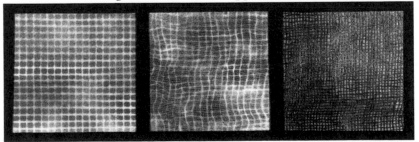

There is another bonus from using spray paint on both canvas and scrim. Put a piece of fabric behind and you get a lovely background to stitch on. The regular squares were sprayed through rug canvas and the distorted ones through coarse scrim. The last illustration shows the medium-weave scrim painted.

Experimenting with fabrics

A day of sticking – Try sticking fabrics and threads on a heavier base material. PVC water-soluble glue is ideal for this. The collage may take some hours to dry but will then be stiff enough to hold its shape and quite easy to work on a frame. It is an excellent base for free embroidery.

The first photograph shows the glued fabric and the second a similar piece after it has been embroidered. It was great fun to stitch; mounted and framed it looks exciting enough to hang on a wall. It was created in quite a random way. If one wanted to think more in terms of the design element, it has a lovely flowing Art Nouveau look about it and the technique would be a good way of designing a landscape or seascape.

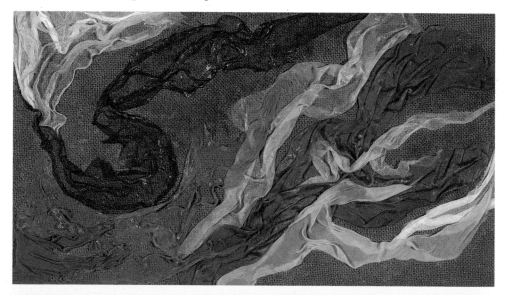

Fireworks – the bonfire at St Stephen's Coombe, Cornwall, was as large as the village was small. Christina was there with the woolly hat and James who likes red. It was a cold night but the bonfire kept us warm and we squealed with delight at every firework and sparkler! The smell of hot jacket potatoes greeted us when we got home, and I sat and dreamed about an embroidery.

I decided to work *Fireworks* as glittering patterns, rather than as a picture of the scene. Until now I had dismissed the possibility of working cross stitch on transparent fabric because of the problem of the threads showing at the back between stitches. But with some lateral thinking I decided to make use of this very factor. I carried out a few trials (working a cross and carrying the thread onto the next stitch so that it showed as a line) on several transparent fabrics. I finally chose black tarlatan and stitched with metallic threads, silver, gold and some colours. The tarlatan showed the lines most clearly whereas nylon blurred them too much. It was certainly a different way of working – care had to be taken to darn in each end of threads as I did not want them to stick out as spikes. The work is backed with bright navy blue fabric.

Night Sky – is rich with bands of silk velvet and stitching. Stars were added later (page 44).

Rosemary Jarvis's notebook

Rosemary is a painter who took the City & Guilds examination in embroidery. Here are some designs from the notebook prepared for the final assessment. It is very exciting to see how she works from first impressions to stitches. I have chosen the subjects which she interpreted freely in cross stitch.

Coastal Path in Winter – the sketch is in crayon and bursts with energy and colour. The background fabric of the embroidery was painted with a colour wash and stitched with many threads including silver.

Meadows – the impression was done with a sponge, a technique Rosemary says she uses more and more. The effect has a strength which immediately relates to fabric and thread.

Winter Cabbage – the design was worked out in tissue paper and as a crayon drawing.

A rich interpretation in stitches. This piece shows the value of using a window viewfinder. It cuts away loose edges and concentrates attention on one strong area.

Christine's Prayer Panel – here are some of the preliminary designs which Rosemary did for the panel reproduced overleaf. Her hand-written notes are interesting.

A detailed collage was the final stage of preparation. It shows the colours, tones and also the moving quality of light she wanted to capture.

City & Guilds work: two panels

Two beautiful cross stitch panels worked by advanced students for their final assessment in the embroidery examination.

'This panel was sparked off by some striking stained glass in a modern Norwegian church. I decided to explore the feeling of light falling through glass. The idea was to use all the colours of the spectrum (which appear in glass) in what was basically a "blue" panel.

'I printed rows of small rectangles in varying strengths of blue, green and yellow dye onto calico, using a piece of plastic foam. Next I applied small frayed-out rectangles of plain and printed fabrics, using Bondaweb (a two-sided iron-on adhesive sheet). Finally, I worked free cross stitch to blend in the rectangles and printed areas, using wools, cotton, perle, metallics, shiny rayon and silk, providing both depth and highlights.

'And the title? Christine and her family were in a time of great darkness and despair, and while I worked on this panel my prayers joined with many. As light came into their situation where before all had appeared "blue" and dark, areas now became vivid and alive with brightness and clarity – as in the glass window.'

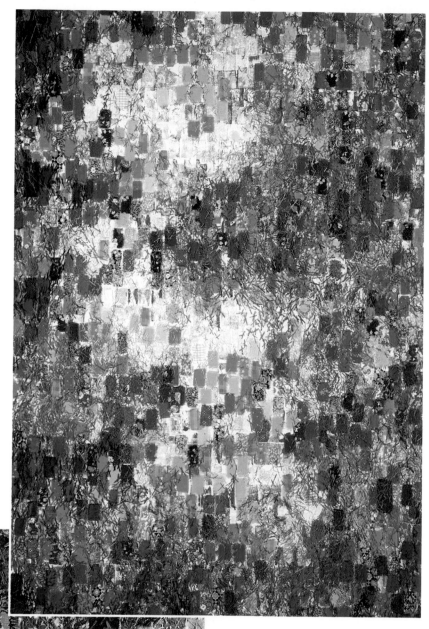

Christine's Prayer Panel
by Rosemary Jarvis

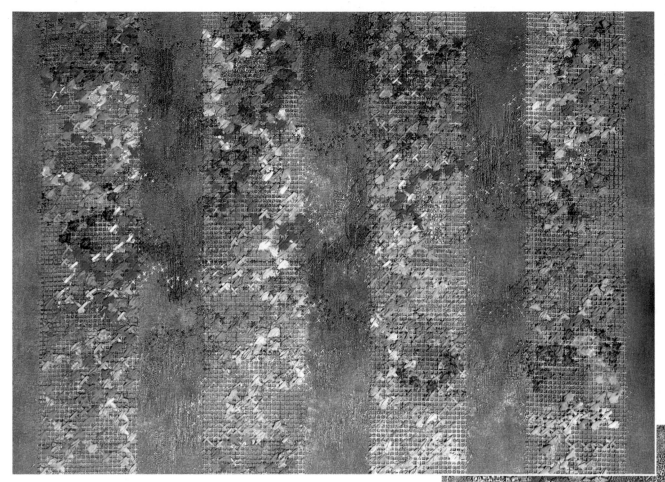

'I have been inspired by gardens for some time and felt that I would like to recreate a herbaceous border in a fairly abstract manner.

'I started with photographs of two different gardens which were of a different scale. I cut both photographs into strips so that one could be worked on a large scale on rug canvas and the other in machine and hand stitching on a linen union background.

'I decided to work in a grid formation to echo the lines of the rug canvas; so, using a rectangular piece of car sponge, I painted both the rug canvas and the linen with Dylon Color-fun paint. I worked free cross stitch on the canvas using torn strips of fabric, knitting tape and nylon organza. Then I worked areas of cable stitch on the linen with the sewing machine.

'My next job was to integrate both areas so that some of the hard edges of the rug canvas were lost. I did this in colours to blend in with the background.

'Finally, I put in the small red cross stitches to represent the bright splashes of colour that one sees in a herbaceous border. I used red as this would make the overall green of the picture sparkle with life.'

Cross Stitch Panel
by Julia Barton

67

Getting to know a subject: The sea

Readers will know from the earlier page of drawings what started me off on the sea! Some pieces of work seem complete in themselves but others lead us on and my first sketch of the sea certainly did that to me. The subject has endless fascination. There are so many ways it can be expressed. Sea in a quiet mood, sea in a storm, sea at night, sea creeping up the beach and sea as described by Coleridge:

> The water like a witch's oil
> Burnt green and blue and white.

I jot down word descriptions as I think of them, collect photographs and pictures of the sea and treasures from the seashore to have round me ... There is a long way to go yet!

A Rolling Heaving Sea – I dyed some silk a soft grey-blue. I then worked out guidelines on paper for this more complicated sea, just as in my first sample, and carried on through every stage exactly as I had done before. As I was working on fine silk and I knew the tacked guidelines would be in for some weeks I was anxious that holes would not be left when tacking was removed from the silk. To prevent this, I used a very fine needle and thread. When it came to removal, I snipped each stitch and gently pulled out the bits with tweezers. There were holes but silk is a natural fabric – with the help of a little steaming the holes disappeared.

The embroidery was worked on a frame. Though the shape and size of the stitching has to move in a free-flowing way it was a controlled piece of work that needed constant thought.

Two seascapes – both had a little help from paint. The fabric of the first embroidery was sprayed with an airbrush. The picture was then developed with cords and stitches to give a stylised view of the sea. The second seascape was painted on silk. Instead of stitching the painted area, I decided to carry the lines of the sea across and to stitch on the mount. The main problem with this exercise was the need to get the lines to meet accurately.

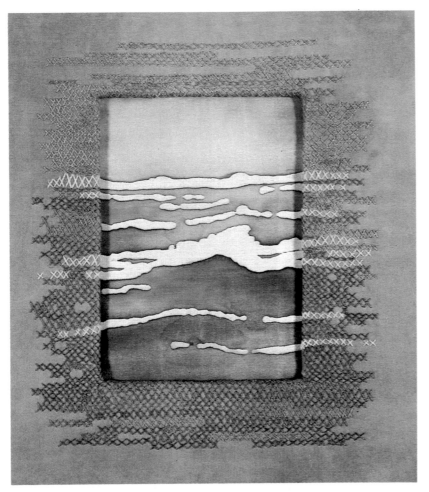

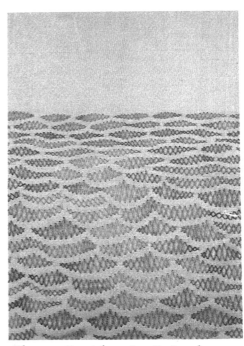

Choppy Sea (above) – I visualised this as an early morning sea with the sun glinting on choppy little waves that are riffled by the breeze. It is stitched in a single thread of stranded cotton in four or five colours.

Sea Hanging – this was a new idea and began my interest in what I now think of as 'making the background fabric'. I painted the base material not knowing at the time whether it would show through in places, and frayed a very long fringe so that the length could be decided at the end. I kept all the unravelled threads, they were to prove invaluable later. The work was to hang from a piece of driftwood that was not straight. I left plenty of material at the top so that I could adjust the length of the straps. I then set about dyeing my fabrics and threads in several bowls of cold-water dye with mixtures from blues to greens. I used a variety of materials: silk, pure cotton, cotton mixture, rayon and synthetic fabrics. They all took up the dyes differently and at different speeds. Each strip was torn and all the edges frayed differently. You need to dye twice the quantity you think you will need as it is necessary to have a lot of choice to ease the colours from one to another comfortably.

The weaver, Anni Albors, said, 'Growing is the thing – not the finished product. You have to take time and listen slowly to what grows out of the material.' This sea hanging did grow and changed very much as I worked at it and enjoyed it.

The stitches play a vital part, their colours and movement affect each piece of fabric differently. The silk has very delicate wrinkles and bubbles, the cotton puckers a little, nylon frays nicely and lies flat. The textural differences as well as the colours help to create the overall effect. The shore at the bottom is stitched and overstitched and has a movement of sand in it.

When I thought the hanging was finished, I backed it, hung it on the driftwood and tidied away my bits. Just one thing kept niggling at me which I tried to ignore as I got on with other work. Whenever I came near the hanging it was certainly speaking to me! The trouble lay at the bottom edge where I had pulled out threads to make a fringe: it was straight and this spoiled the surging movement of the whole embroidery. Having fortunately kept the unravelled threads I could weave these back at the top of the fringe to make the edge irregular. Then I stitched over it. We now live peacefully together.

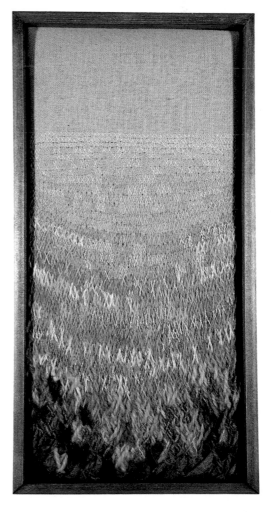

Calm Sea at Early Evening – this embroidery is on natural-coloured silk and stitched with fine silk threads. The stitching is simple and regular, the work depending on colour for its impact. It is mounted on brown silk.

A Textured Sea – I dyed the background material and some of the threads a pale turquoise – and was later to paint the frame in the same colour. I had to choose the weave of the background fabric carefully. It had to be close enough for the sky to be smooth but with some 'give' in it so that I could pull through strips of fabric and thick wool at the bottom. I did manage to stitch with the heavy threads by using a very thick sharp needle and a great deal of patience. As usual I worked on a frame, as this piece of work would have become distorted if it had been attempted in the hand. You can well imagine that stitching with strips of fabric made the back of the work bulky. When mounting, I stuck a sheet of foam plastic on the mounting board before stretching the embroidery – this absorbed the bumps.

More scenes

American Holiday

This was our first visit to America and old friendships took us to the southern states. At long last there was an opportunity to visit New Orleans, where we saw Preservation Hall and the Mississippi – later the Grand Canyon and San Francisco. I cannot say that, after just a month, America was easy to put into stitches. So much is atmosphere and friendliness – it is intangible. You cannot embroider, 'Have a nice day!' but that sums up for me the feel of the country. I indulged myself and tried to give a mixture of 'flavours' in my *Postcard from America.*

Grand Canyon – a large piece of embroidery. It presented problems and took a long time to do but I enjoyed every stitch. It was a constant reminder of a lovely holiday and the thrilling sight of the Canyon. That day was something special and I wanted to capture it.

All the threads for this embroidery were dyed. It was quite difficult to decide the 'weight' of colour of the first row of stitching as I wanted the work to come forward and recede in a soft but positive way. I began by working just the centre section but found that the changes in colour were so slight and subtle that I would never be able to pick them up again when embroidering at the sides – so I had to frame up all three sections and work right across.

I tried mounting the panels on different colours – each evoked a different atmosphere: grey-blue made it look more open and cooler.

More scenes

Trees through the seasons
A group of trees designed in cut paper to depict spring, autumn and winter. The tree in winter was the hardest to express: all designs were worked out in coloured paper and newsprint.

Spring

Winter

Autumn

The spring tree embroidered.

74

It occurred to me as I assembled this page how much of the work can be seen to have developed directly from the little early experiments that were carried out to express different moods and movements in stitches (see page 16).

A Fishing Place – this is a scene that I had painted and crayoned earlier and now recreated in painted fabric, threads and pieces of material. For large areas of background, small pieces of differently coloured materials were tacked on. One of the hardest things to gauge in an embroidery like this is when to stop. You have to go on stitching for a long time if you want to create a textured effect and then, quite suddenly, you have overstitched and it is very difficult to unpick. I try not to stitch for too long when I am nearing this stage – I leave it propped up for a bit and come back and look at it afresh.

Wind in the Grass – this embroidery tried to catch the riffling movement of a breeze stirring a field of grass.

A Quiet Scene – I spend a lot of time thinking about how to make texture and movement and colour. Then one day I wanted to capture something quite different – space and silence. This scene was the result.

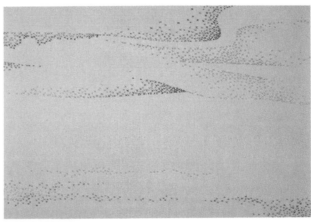

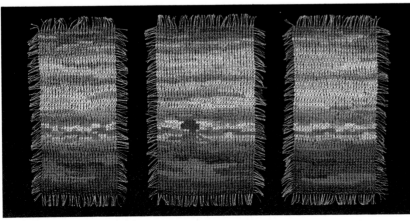

Sunset – worked on scrim which was in one piece originally. The rectangles were carefully tacked out to be identical and well spaced to allow for cutting and fraying. I stitched exactly to the tacking lines so that when fabric was frayed the edges remained secure. The three pieces were mounted on dark blue velvet.

Cornish Hedge – The traditional high Cornish hedges all have as a base a stone wall. Because of the lush growth in Cornwall it soon becomes completely covered with grasses, creepers and wild flowers. There are so many flowers, especially in the spring, that on warm days there is always the droning of bees and the whole hedge is alive with insects and other animal life. It's warm and sheltered at the bottom but usually blowy at the top!

a

b

c
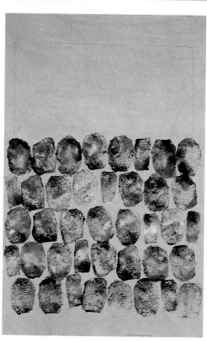

d

a My first drawings were for my own pleasure, not as designs for embroidery. But with my photographs they were useful reference to have by me.

b A freer painting of the hedge with stitching in mind. I used a sponge and a large dry brush.

c With some shaped pieces of sponge dipped in semi-mixed paint I printed the stones that form the base of a hedge.

d I painted a scudding Cornish sky and stuck bits of fabric on my wall.

My first Cornish Hedge completed. I enjoyed every stitch but felt that the result was rather photographic.

Detail of first hedge.

A second Cornish Hedge – While I was still happy with the subject, I decided to work it again. I put away all my drawings and photographs, chose a lovely piece of linen and stitched straight into it with no preparation. I could not have tackled it 'cold' like this if I had not been steeped in the subject. This time I tried to make the stitches and a few pieces of painted scrim express it all.

After some hours of solid stitching, I ran into a problem: the top right-hand area had become flat and overstitched. Eventually I came up with a solution. A small piece of irregularly-shaped green net, lightly stitched, changed the tempo sufficiently. When I had finished the hedge I also recreated a windy sky. It worked well in cross stitch but because the hedge was 'busy' I found it was essential to leave the sky empty and calm, so I unpicked these stitches.

Conclusion

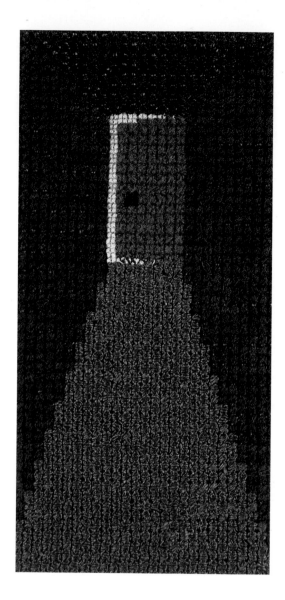

I was in a hall full of doors at the beginning of the book and I am still in a hall full of doors, but more of them are now open.

To live with one stitch for several years is an enthralling experience. At the end of that time you might expect that ideas would be slowing down but it is the reverse – the experience becomes more absorbing. Every piece of work indicates how it could be done better or differently and that is the excitement. There is always the next piece of work clamouring for attention. The trouble is that there is no way that fingers can keep up with ideas!

If this notebook interests you, thread up your needles and push open some more doors. Cross stitch has not been as widely explored as a lot of stitches and it deserves the skill and imagination of many more embroiderers.

Several paintings and samples of stitching were considered before a choice was made for the final embroidery.

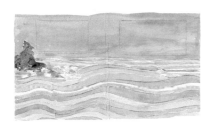

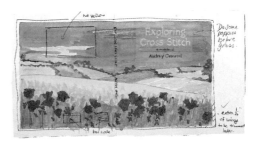

Book list

Through lack of space I have been unable to give practical information on vital subjects such as stretching and mounting finished work. To give instructions on this and a whole range of embroidery and design techniques I would recommend:
Needlework School, by the Embroiderers' Guild Practical Study Group (Windward)

To inspire you to work adventurously in colour:
Embroidery and Colour, by Constance Howard (Batsford)

The following two books by textile artists show how their excitement and inspiration are harnessed into tangible forms:
The Art of Zandra Rhodes, by Zandra Rhodes and Anne Knight (Cape)
Glorious Knitting, by Kaffe Fassett (Century)

A more advanced book for those who want to study design:
Basic Design: the dynamics of visual form, by Maurice de Sausmarez (Herbert Press)

Two magazines to keep you up to date with craft activities:
Embroidery, a quarterly magazine that has articles on modern and historical embroidery and information on exhibitions, books, courses, day schools, etc. It is published for the Embroiderers' Guild and can be ordered through newsagents or obtained by post from Apartment 41A, Hampton Court Palace, East Molesey, Surrey KT8 9AU
Crafts, a bi-monthly magazine covering all crafts. Very stimulating, carries an article on textiles in most issues. Gives information on exhibitions, specialist shops, books and courses, It can be obtained through newsagents or by post from Crafts Magazine, 8 Waterloo Place, London SW1Y 4AT

Addresses

The Embroiderers' Guild
Apartment 41, Hampton Court Palace, East Molesey, Surrey KT8 9AU
Membership is open to anyone interested in embroidery. The Guild has a unique collection of embroideries and specialist books, runs a wide range of classes and holds exhibitions of modern and historical work. It can supply addresses of local branches thoughout the UK.

The Royal School of Needlework
Apartment 38, Hampton Court Palace, East Molesey, Surrey KT8 9AU
Undertakes embroidery commissions, restores valuable embroideries and lace, runs courses and has a shop selling a wide range of embroidery materials.

My 'Aladdin's Cave' in London for fabrics is:
Boverick Fabrics Ltd.
16 Berwick Street, London W1V 4HP
Go right through to the back shop. It is here, in a packed room, that you will find all the exciting theatrical fabrics.

Plasterers' scrim can be obtained from suppliers of sculpture materials, such as
Alec Tiranti Ltd
27 Warren Street, London W1P 5DG
70 High Street, Theale, Berks. RG7 5AR

Fabric transfer paints are supplied by post from
B. A. Marketing (Leicester)
8 Latimer Street, Leicester LE3 0QE